JOURNEY TO ADVENTURE!

LEVEL 5, THEME 1

Integrated Theme Test Record

Student ____ Date ___________

STUDENT PROFILE					
	Part Scores:	Excellent Progress	Good Progress	Some Progress	Needs Improvement
Part 1: Reading Strategies •self-question •monitor	Items 1–2	7–8	5–6	3–4	0–2
Part 2: Comprehension •sequence of events •categorize and classify •text organization	Items 3–7 (written)	17–20	13–16	10–12	0–9
	Items 8–12 (multiple-choice)	20	16	8–12	0–4
Part 3: Word Skills •base words and inflected forms •suffixes meaning "someone who" •classifying/categorizing	Items 13–17	15	12	9	0–6
Part 4: Writing and Language Writing Fluency	Item 18 Fluency	20	15	10	0–5
Proofreading •spelling long vowels •kinds of sentences, subjects/ predicates, run-on sentences	Item 19 Language	8–9	6–7	4–5	0–3
Writing Skills •writing a sentence	Items 20–21 Writing Skills	8		4	0
Part 5: Self-Assessment (optional) •self-assessment/reflection •developing preferences	Home Letter	Scoring of Self-Assessment is not recommended. Evaluate answers for evidence of metacognitive growth.			

Total Score

____

- ☐ Excellent (90–100)
- ☐ Good (75–89)
- ☐ Satisfactory (60–74)
- ☐ Needs Improvement (0–59)

Additional Comments _____________________________

____

____

____

Test taken independently ☐

Test taken with partial support ☐

Test taken with full support ☐

JOURNEY TO ADVENTURE!

In Journey to Adventure! you read about real people and fictional characters who faced challenges on land, at sea, in air, and in space.

Now you will read an article about an adventure deep inside the earth. Included with the article is a short selection about the cave that the author visits.

There are questions to answer before, during, and after your reading. You may go back to the selections to help you answer the questions.

1 READING STRATEGIES

1. **Self-Question** Before you read, look over the titles, headings, and pictures. Write a question that you think will be answered as you read.

____

____

____

____

____

Down the Rope to Adventure

by Mark L. Taylor
from *Ranger Rick* magazine

I'm a newspaper reporter and I love to explore caves. So when I got a chance to explore Lechuguilla Cave *and* write a story about it, I couldn't believe my luck. That is, until I saw the entrance—90 feet (27 m) straight *down*!

My heart pounded with excitement as I slid down a long rope into the deep pit. What a wild start to a trip!

At the bottom I joined the other cavers who were going with me into the cave. The trip leader was a scientist named Barbara am Ende. She led us to a skinny metal tunnel. *This is the weirdest way into a cave that I've ever seen,* I thought.

One by one we wiggled our way feet-first down the tiny tunnel. Beyond were the wonders of Lechuguilla.

Water poured in after a storm, so this caver got a shower as she slid down the rope.

BONES, BELLS, AND STRAWS

For the next 13 hours we moved about in total darkness. We had only our small headlamps to light the way. But I wasn't worried about getting lost. We were following a map that had been made by earlier explorers.

Compared to caves in the eastern United States, Lechuguilla is dry and warm. No slogging through mud and muck! But small amounts of water do seep into Lechuguilla from above ground. This water mixes with a soft rock called *limestone*. Together they create some of the cave formations. *Stalactites* (stuh-LACK-tites) hang from the ceiling, and *stalagmites* (stuh-LAG-mites) grow from the floor.

In the weak light of my headlamp, I could see small stalactites here and there. But so far I hadn't seen anything special. Then we came to the "Liberty Bell." *I'd hate to have **that** stalactite fall on my head*, I thought as I looked at the huge shape looming overhead.

Next, we turned down a short, skinny passage. It was crowded with tiny stalactites called *soda straws*. Even a gentle touch can break a soda straw. So we turned sideways and moved carefully past them. Barbara found another surprise beyond the soda straws — the skeleton of an ancient bobcat. She said it must have gotten lost inside the cave and died there thousands of years ago.

Cavers, such as this man climbing beside the "Liberty Bell," sometimes explore in their bare feet. Boots can easily break delicate formations.

Stop here and answer Question 2. Then continue reading.

2. **Monitor** In the selection, what technique does the
author use to help you know what he is thinking?

____

____

____

____

Rubric Score for Items 1–2 ________

8

ROOMS OF WONDER

Back in the main passage, we came to what looked like a dead end. But then we looked down: In the light of our headlamps, the passage dropped away into blackness. Our map called this pit "Boulder Falls." To go any farther, we would have to drop by rope through 15 stories of air.

Barbara looped an extra-long climbing rope around several big boulders and tied it. Next, she clipped the rope into special climbing equipment that would help her drop slowly into the pit. Then she gripped the rope and stepped off the ledge.

One by one, the other cavers dropped into the dark. Finally, it was my turn. As I let myself down the rope, I gently bounced against a rock wall. *Not too bad yet,* I thought calmly. Then the wall disappeared and I was dangling in midair. Far below, the other cavers' headlamps glowed like distant fireflies. Inch by inch, I slid down as the rope spun me slowly round and round. Finally my toes touched the floor of the pit.

That scary drop left us in the middle of a room so big I couldn't see the walls. From there, we scrambled down a slope of jumbled boulders. At the bottom we saw one of the cave's spookiest sights.

We were in another enormous room. In the feeble glow of our headlamps, huge white blocks seemed to float in the inky darkness ahead of us. Some blocks were the size of a small car; others were as big as a house.

Cavers call this eerie room "Glacier Bay," and Barbara explained why. We were standing on a 30-foot (9-m) thick layer of a mineral called *gypsum* (JIP-sum). The white blocks had broken off the edge of the gypsum layer, sort of the way icebergs break off glaciers.

UP FROM UNDERGROUND

Beyond Glacier Bay are miles of passages and more gigantic rooms. But we wouldn't explore them on this trip. It was time for us to head back.

Now that the excitement was over, I felt tired. But we still had to scramble and climb for many hours before we'd reach the surface.

When we were close to the entrance, I heard moaning. *What's that?* I wondered. I shivered as a wind from deep in the cave blew against my back. Then I realized, *That's the wind moaning!*

Sure enough, the closer we got to the entrance, the harder the wind blew and the louder it moaned. The wind almost pushed us through the tiny tunnel, as if the cave wanted us to leave.

Finally we came to the entrance pit and that last long rope. As I climbed, I could see stars twinkling in the sky. I was exhausted, hungry . . . and *happy*. I had explored part of this wild underground wonderland!

Climbing down the crumbly rock of "Glacier Bay" is tricky. This caver (above) searches for a place big enough–and strong enough–for his next step.

Lechuguilla Cave

from *Ranger Rick* magazine

They call it Lechuguilla (lech-uh-GHEE-yeh) Cave. This super cave is tucked away in a little canyon in Carlsbad Caverns National Park, New Mexico. It's full of deep pits, hidden rooms, miles and miles of dark passages—and formations that are found in few other caves.

Many formations are made of minerals that look like snow. And they are as fragile as a snowflake too. For instance, a caver can't pet this "bunny" (1) or put an ornament on this "Christmas tree" (2). And no one could chew these globs of "bubble gum" (4). One touch would shatter such fragile formations.

Far from the cave's entrance cavers enter the huge "Chandelier Ballroom" (3). A few other caves have chandeliers, but none are as big as those in Lechuguilla.

3.

1.

2. 4.

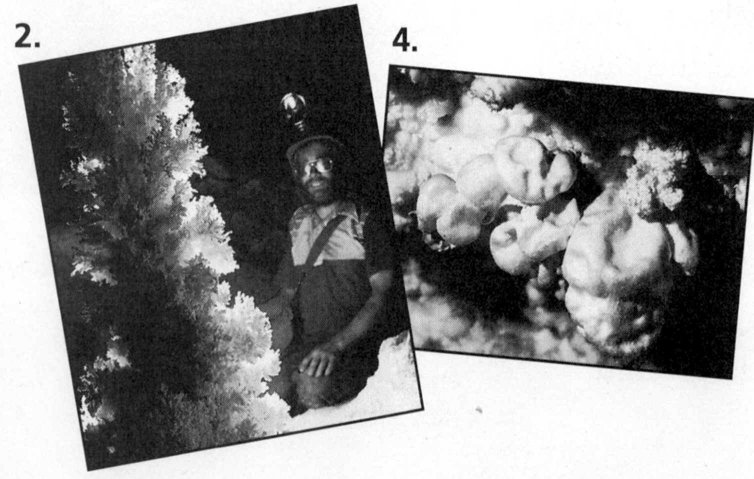

Only a few people have seen the treasures deep inside Lechuguilla. These sights are their reward for crawling and climbing for hours in the unexplored passages and rooms of this super cave.

COMPREHENSION

Write your answers to these questions.

3. Tell what kind of person you think the author is, and how you know this about him.

____

____

____

____

____

4. What kinds of equipment did the cavers use, and what did they use these things for? Complete the chart below.

Type of Equipment	What the Equipment Is Used For
a. Map	
b.	To keep the cavers from falling when lowering into the pit
c.	

5. Why does the author use "Bones, Bells, and Straws" as a heading on page 5?

____

____

____

____

____

6. Describe two unusual things the explorers saw in the cave.

1. ____

____

____

2. ____

____

____

7. List the steps the explorers took to get down Boulder Falls.

Step 1: ____

____

Step 2: ____

____

Step 3: ____

____

Rubric Score for Items 3–7 _______
20

8. How is Lechuguilla Cave different from caves in
   the eastern United States?

   ○ a. It has stalactites.
   ○ b. Cave paintings are found in Lechuguilla.
   ○ c. It is dry and warm.
   ○ d. It is wet and muddy.

9. What made exploring the cave difficult?

   ○ a. It was cold and very windy.
   ○ b. There were dangerous icebergs breaking off
         from the glaciers.
   ○ c. There were many loose rocks that broke off.
   ○ d. It was dark and had many steep passages.

10. Why do the cavers call the big room "Glacier Bay?"

    ○ a. It has many icebergs that have broken off a
          large glacier.
    ○ b. It is cold and icy like a glacier.
    ○ c. There is a thick layer of mineral that looks like
          a glacier.
    ○ d. The rocks were left by a glacier.

11. Reread the text beneath the heading "Up from
Underground." What would be another good heading
to describe this part of the article?

- a.   Exploring a Big Cave
- b.   The End of the Trip
- c.   A Dead End
- d.   Glacier Bay

12. When did the author feel a strong wind?

- a.   when he was near the cave entrance
- b.   after he moved past the soda straws
- c.   before he dropped down Boulder Falls
- d.   when he reached Glacier Bay

Score for Items 8–12 (x4) _______

20

3 WORD SKILLS

The sentences below come from the selections you just read. Use what you know about figuring out new words to help you select the correct answer.

13. *She led us to a skinny metal tunnel.* This is the <u>weirdest</u> way into a cave that I've ever seen, *I thought.*

    What does the author think about the entrance to the cave?
    - ○ a. It is not as strange as others he has seen.
    - ○ b. It is odder than some other entrances he has seen.
    - ○ c. It is the most unusual entrance he has ever seen.
    - ○ d. It is a peculiar entrance.

14. *Far from the cave's entrance cavers enter the huge "<u>Chandelier</u> Ballroom."*

    Which one of these is similar to a *chandelier*?
    - ○ a. a flashlight
    - ○ b. an overhead light
    - ○ c. a lamp
    - ○ d. a night-light

15. Not too bad yet, *I thought calmly. Then the wall disappeared and I was <u>dangling</u> in midair.*

    What was the author doing?
    - ○ a. He was about to hang.
    - ○ b. He was hanging from a rope.
    - ○ c. He was falling down a slope.
    - ○ d. He had been hanging from a rope.

16. *At the bottom I joined the other <u>cavers</u> who were going*
with me into the cave.

Whom was the author joining in the cave?
- ○ a. people who write about caves
- ○ b. animals that live in caves
- ○ c. people who explore caves
- ○ d. people who are afraid of caves

17. *Many formations are made of minerals that look like snow.*
And they are as <u>fragile</u> as a snowflake too.

What are the formations like?
- ○ a. They are easily damaged or broken.
- ○ b. They are strong and sturdy.
- ○ c. They are very cold.
- ○ d. They are formed in the winter.

Score for Items 13–17 (x3) _______

15

4 WRITING AND LANGUAGE

18. Write one or two paragraphs about one of the
topics below.

    a. Tell about a real-life adventure that has happened to
you. Include details that make the adventure seem real
to the reader. Tell how you met the challenges of the
adventure.

    b. Describe an adventure that you would like to
experience. Explain what you expect your adventure
would be like. What would you do to help meet the
challenge of this adventure?

Rubric Score for Item 18 (x5) ________

20

19. Read the article below. Find and correct nine errors. Use what you know about proofreading to make your corrections in the article. The examples may help you. There are four spelling errors and five errors in forming sentences.

Spelunking Safely

Last year I went caving with my Boy Scout troop. Our leader, Mr. Schultz, an experienced spelunker. He told us that caving is an exciting but very dangerous hobby. For weeks before we went, Mr. Schultz taught us all about the sayfety rules that spelunkers follo when exploring a cave.

Cavers have special safety equipment that they use when spelunking! They wear hardhats and heavy suits to protect themselves against sharp rock formations. Also, cavers always carry two sources of lite. They attach a headlamp to their hardhats, and they carry a flashlight. Helps cavers navigate the dark cave.

The most important rule to remember is never to explore caves alone cavers always explore in groups so there is help if there is danger.

Score for Item 19 _________

9

Choose the group of words that is a sentence.

20. ○ a.   Are damp and dark.
     ○ b.   Many animals live in caves.
     ○ c.   Where the sun never.
     ○ d.   Unusual rock formations.

21. ○ a.   Special climbing equipment.
     ○ b.   Sliding down the long rope.
     ○ c.   Be careful when exploring a cave.
     ○ d.   Keeps the caver from falling.

Score for Items 20–21 (x4) _________

8

5 HOME LETTER

Write a letter to a friend or relative. Your answer should show that you have thought about what you have read.

Date ________________

Dear ________________,

We have just finished the theme called Journey to Adventure! I learned about real and imaginary adventures and the challenges people face.

My favorite selection in this theme was ________________

____

because ________________

____

One thing I learned about facing challenges is ________________

____

All the adventurers I read about are similar because ________________

____

____

____

Sincerely,

____

5 HOME LETTER

IN THE WILD
LEVEL 5, THEME 2
Integrated Theme Test Record

Student ____ Date ____________

	Part Scores:	Excellent Progress	Good Progress	Some Progress	Needs Improvement
Part 1: Reading Strategies •self-question •predict/infer	Items 1–2	7–8	5–6	3–4	0–2
Part 2: Comprehension •author's viewpoint, fact and opinion •making inferences	Items 3–7 (written)	17–20	13–16	10–12	0–9
•topic, main idea, supporting details, and summarizing	Items 8–12 (multiple-choice)	20	16	8–12	0–4
Part 3: Word Skills •homophones •suffixes •prefixes	Items 13–17	15	12	9	0–6
Part 4: Writing and Language Writing Fluency	Item 18 Fluency	20	15	10	0–5
Proofreading •spelling vowel + *r* sounds •singular and plural nouns, possessive nouns, common and proper nouns	Item 19 Language	8–9	6–7	4–5	0–3
Writing Skills •combining sentences: compound sentences, appositives	Items 20–21 Writing Skills	8		4	0
Part 5: Self-Assessment (optional) •self-assessment/reflection •developing preferences	Home Letter	Scoring of Self-Assessment is not recommended. Evaluate answers for evidence of metacognitive growth.			

STUDENT PROFILE

Total Score
____

- ☐ Excellent (90–100)
- ☐ Good (75–89)
- ☐ Satisfactory (60–74)
- ☐ Needs Improvement (0–59)

Additional Comments _____________________

____

____

Test taken independently ☐

Test taken with partial support ☐

Test taken with full support ☐

In the
WILD

In the Wild contained stories about the wonders of the animal kingdom and about relationships between humans and animals.

Now you will read a true story about a baboon who helped run a railroad. You will also read a short article about baboons in the wild.

There are questions to answer before, during, and after your reading. You may go back to the selections to help you answer the questions.

1 READING STRATEGIES

1. **Self-Question** Preview the two selections by looking at each title and the pictures. Write a question that you think will be answered as you read.

____

____

____

____

____

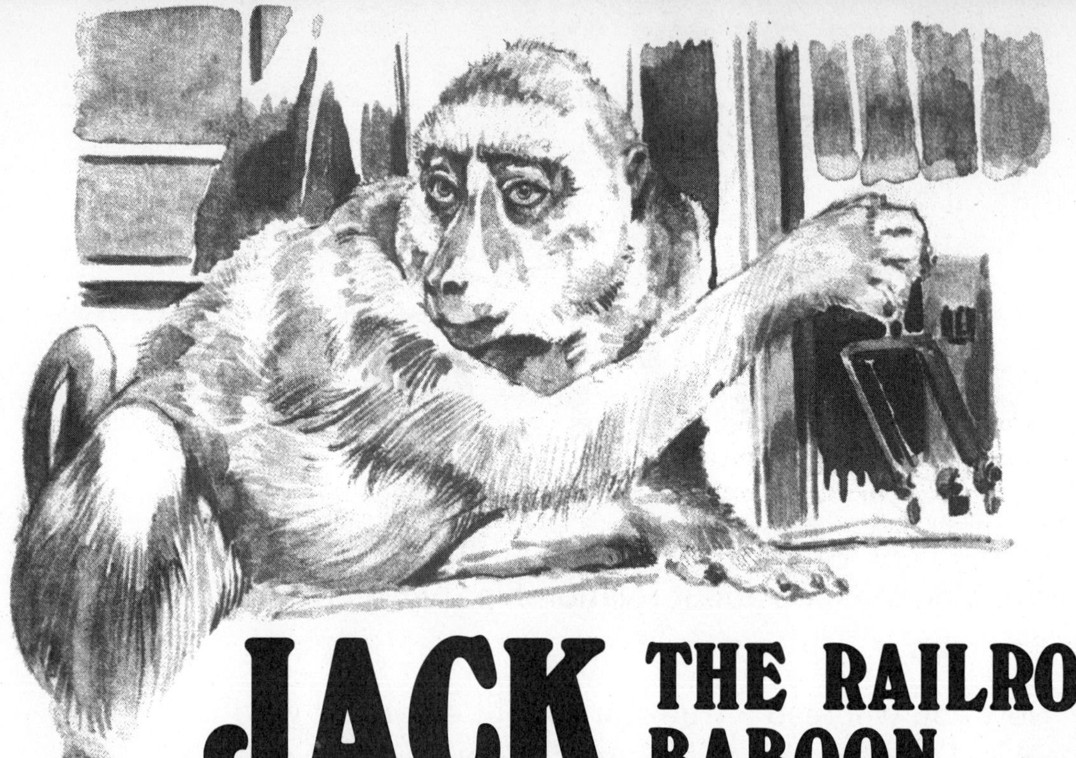

JACK THE RAILROAD BABOON

by Ken Fleming
from *Cricket* magazine

Have you ever wondered what it must be like to run a railroad? Setting the red, yellow, and green signal lights to stop, slow down, or speed up the trains, or throwing the switches so the trains change to the right tracks. A mistake could cost millions of dollars in damages or even people's lives.

Sounds like a big job, but from 1881 to 1890 a 150-pound chacma, or pig-tailed baboon, ran a switching complex in South Africa.

His friend and partner, James Wylde, was a railroad worker who had lost his legs during a job accident in 1877. He became signalman at the Uitenhage Station near Port Elizabeth, which is centrally located between the five major port cities and the gold and diamond mines of South Africa.

The switching tower oversaw a network of main lines that connected the cities to small towns and villages in the jungle. James's job was to transfer approaching trains to the correct tracks and to their proper destinations.

But James Wylde had one problem that was hard to cope with. He lived in a lonely, tumble-down cabin near the station and he had no neighbors to talk to.

One summer afternoon in 1881, James went shopping at a noisy and crowded local street market. As he rolled his wheelchair past a man who sold animals and brightly feathered birds, a small wooden cage caught James's eye. A gray-black baby baboon, with its tiny pink hands clutching the cage bars, screeched loudly.

James bought the frightened animal and took it home. He coaxed the little baboon from the cramped cage, then tossed the cage into the fireplace. He fed the baby some warmed goat's milk and gave it a bath. Then James held the little creature in his arms and softly talked it to sleep.

During the year that followed, James was happier than he had been in years. He talked all the time to the growing baboon he had named Jack. The loss of his legs didn't matter as much to James any more. Jack had brought hope back into James's life.

James only had one worry. Maybe Jack should go back to the jungle. Am I being selfish in keeping him from his natural environment? he asked himself. One day James opened the cabin door and rolled his wheelchair to the back of the room. He watched as the baboon sat in the open doorway. Jack stared into the starry night while James waited anxiously. Then Jack yawned, stood up, and closed the door. He climbed onto James's lap and fell asleep.

Stop here and answer Question 2. Then continue reading.

READING STRATEGIES (continued)

2. **Predict/Infer** How do you think Jack the Railroad Baboon might help James?

____

____

____

____

Rubric Score for Items 1–2 _______

8

As Jack got older, he began to help with the chores. Jack was a fast learner. He pumped water from a well and carried the buckets of water inside. Soon he was tending the vegetable garden and doing the dishes, too.

James paid him a salary: one tin of cookies and two chocolate bars a week. Jack was especially fond of the candy. He tucked it in his large cheek pouches to eat later.

At the switching tower, Jack found more ways to help. He swept up with a broom and washed the many windows. A special key that hung from a peg on the wall had to be given to the locomotive drivers to open remote switches farther up the line. When Jack heard a train coming, he took the key down and waited by the tracks. He would jump aboard the slow-moving engines, deliver the key, and then hop off. On the train's return, he would get the key back and put it on its peg again.

Jack also learned to help with the signal flags and lanterns. Soon James could name a signal, and Jack would wave the proper color.

Finally James decided to train the baboon to help with switching tracks, too. Jack's bright eyes followed James as he worked the tall, heavy control levers. James called each of them by number. Then he repeated each number and touched each switch. These lessons took hours, but finally Jack could pull the correct one every time.

James tested Jack every day. Weeks went by before he decided to let Jack switch a train. At first Jack transferred only slow freights, then faster ones.

When the time came to direct a passenger train, James was a bit worried about an accident. He had faith in Jack, but this was a big responsibility. People could be hurt. After a great deal of thought, James decided to trust his partner.

"Red flag, Jack," he shouted. "Yellow flag, pull three." The baboon moved with an expert's ease. "Green flag, Jack."

The passenger train changed tracks and sped on its way.

That was the first of thousands of trains moving accident-free under Jack's control. Jack became so good at the job that he eventually ran the entire signal and switching operation, and James Wylde could remain at home. For nine happy years the partners worked together at the signal station. Then, in 1890, Jack died of tuberculosis.

Not all baboons live with people. The following article tells about many types of baboons and how they usually live.

Baboons

from *The World Book Encyclopedia*

Baboon is a type of large monkey. A baboon has a large head and long, sharp canine teeth, and a muzzle much like that of a dog. A baboon's arms are about as long as its legs. Some baboons have short, stumpy tails, but others have tails more than 2 feet (61 centimeters) long. Male baboons are much larger than the females and have longer canine teeth. Some female baboons weigh as little as 24 pounds (11 kilograms). A male baboon may weigh 90 pounds (41 kilograms).

Baboons live mostly on the ground but sleep in such places as trees or cliffs. Several kinds of baboons live in Africa and southwestern Arabia. These include the *hamadryas* baboon, which lives on the plains and rocky hills of Arabia, Egypt, Ethiopia, and Sudan, and the *chacma* baboon, which inhabits rocky regions and open woodlands in southern Africa. Male hamadryas baboons have long, gray hair on the head and shoulders. Chacma baboons have grayish-brown body hair and a long ruff of hair around the neck. Males occasionally kill mammals and share the meat with other group members.

Baboons eat eggs, fruits, grass, insects, and roots. They can carry food in pouches inside their cheeks.

2 COMPREHENSION

Write your answers to these questions.

3. How does the author feel about the relationship between James and Jack? What clues support your ideas?

4. Why did James toss Jack's cage into the fireplace?

5. Why did James worry that he was being selfish to keep Jack?

6. Describe three ways in which Jack helped James.

____

____

____

____

____

____

7. What did Jack need to learn in order to be able to run the switching complex?

____

____

____

____

____

____

Rubric Score for Items 3–7 ________

20

Choose the best answer and fill in the circle.

8. How can you tell that James loved Jack immediately?

   - ○ a. He taught Jack how to do chores for him.
   - ○ b. He held Jack and talked him to sleep.
   - ○ c. He gave Jack lots of chocolate and cookies.
   - ○ d. He wouldn't let Jack run away.

9. How did James reward Jack for his help?

   - ○ a. He gave Jack Sundays off.
   - ○ b. He let Jack go back to the jungle.
   - ○ c. He paid Jack a salary.
   - ○ d. He sometimes let Jack ride the trains.

10. What did James make Jack do before he let Jack switch passenger trains?

   - ○ a. He made Jack show that he could switch freight trains.
   - ○ b. He made Jack tend the vegetable garden and do the dishes.
   - ○ c. He made Jack run the entire switching station.
   - ○ d. He made Jack show that he could drive the trains.

11. How was Jack similar to most other baboons?

- ○ a. Jack weighed the same as other baboons.
- ○ b. Jack ate mostly eggs, fruits, grass, insects, and roots.
- ○ c. Jack carried food in his cheek pouches.
- ○ d. Jack shared the food he killed with his companion, James.

12. In "Jack the Railroad Baboon," what seems to be the author's opinion about baboons?

- ○ a. They should stay in the wild.
- ○ b. They are very smart.
- ○ c. They are dangerous.
- ○ d. They are a type of large monkey that lives in Africa.

Score for Items 8–12 (x4) ______
20

WORD SKILLS

Read the sentence or sentences. Use what you know about figuring out new words to help you select the correct answer.

13. *Am I being selfish in keeping him from his natural <u>environment</u>? he asked himself.*

    What place did James fear he was keeping the baboon from?
    - ○ a.   the baboon's wooden cage
    - ○ b.   the baboon's home in the jungle
    - ○ c.   the home of the man who sold animals
    - ○ d.   the crowded street market

14. *Jack had brought <u>hope</u> back into James's life.*

    How did Jack make James feel?
    - ○ a.   Jack made James feel hopeless.
    - ○ b.   Jack made James feel hopefully.
    - ○ c.   Jack made James feel like hope.
    - ○ d.   Jack made James feel hopeful.

15. *Soon James could name a signal, and Jack would wave the <u>proper</u> color.*

    After he had learned the signals, what did Jack do?
    - ○ a.   Jack chose the colors proper.
    - ○ b.   Jack chose the colors promptly.
    - ○ c.   Jack chose the colors properly.
    - ○ b.   Jack chose the colors property.

16. *On the train's <u>return</u>, he would get the key back and put it on its peg again.*

When would Jack get the key back?
- ○ a. when the train came back through the station
- ○ b. when the train turned a corner near the station
- ○ c. when he arrived back at James's house
- ○ d. when the train was farther up the line

17. *Chacma baboons have grayish-brown body hair and a long <u>ruff</u> of hair around the neck.*

What does *ruff* mean?
- ○ a. coarse hair around the tail
- ○ b. coarse and thick
- ○ c. long and thick
- ○ d. long, thick hair around the neck

Score for Items 13–17 (x3) _________

15

4 WRITING AND LANGUAGE

18. Write one or two paragraphs about one of the topics below.

    a. James liked having Jack the baboon as a companion. What animal would you like to have as a companion? Explain why.

    b. Do you think wild animals should live in the wild, in a zoo, or as someone's pet? Give reasons for your choice.

____

____

____

____

Rubric Score for Item 18 (x5) _______

20

19. Read the letter below. Find and correct nine errors. Use what you know about proofreading to make your corrections in the letter. The examples may help you. There are three spelling errors, four errors in plurals, and two errors in proper nouns.

435 Falcon Street
Rollingwood, Texas 78746
April 8, 1996

Editor, <u>The Rollingwood Daily News</u>
Rollingwood, Texas 78746

Dear Sir:

Years ago I moved here because of the beautiful hills and trees. My husband and I built a house near a small creek. We grew to love and respect the wild animals that visited our family's property. Birds, rabbits, and deers have shared these woods with us. You can lern a lot about wild creatures when you live near them.

Now, other familys are moving to rollingwood. I feer that this is threatening the animals's natural homes. Trees and bushs are being cut down to build houses. People don't seem to caer if they destroy one home to build another. I urge everyone who cares about animals to come to a meeting on april 19 at City Hall.

Sincerely,

Lorraine Ashworth

Score for Item 19 _________
9

Combine the two sentences below to form a compound sentence.

20. Most bears have dark fur. Polar bears have
white fur.

____

____

____

____

**Combine the two sentences below to form one sentence with
an appositive.**

21. Porcupines use their sharp quills for protection. Porcupines
are a kind of rodent.

____

____

____

____

Score for Items 20–21 (x4) ________

8

5 HOME LETTER

Write a letter to a friend or relative. Your letter should show that you have thought about what you have read.

Date ___________________________

Dear ____ ,

We have just finished our study of In the Wild. This theme is about animals in the wild.

My opinion of this theme is _______________________________

My favorite story in this theme was _______________________________

because _______________________________

The most interesting thing I learned about the relationship between animals and humans is _______________________________

____

____

I became a better reader during this theme by learning

____

____

Sincerely,

____

TRY TO SEE IT MY WAY

LEVEL 5, THEME 3

Integrated Theme Test Record

Student ______________________________________ Date ____________

<table>
<tr><th colspan="6">STUDENT PROFILE</th></tr>
<tr><th></th><th>Part Scores:</th><th>Excellent Progress</th><th>Good Progress</th><th>Some Progress</th><th>Needs Improvement</th></tr>
<tr><td>Part 1: Reading Strategies
•self-question
•monitor</td><td>Items 1–2</td><td>7–8</td><td>5–6</td><td>3–4</td><td>0–2</td></tr>
<tr><td rowspan="2">Part 2: Comprehension
•noting details
•compare and contrast
•predicting outcomes
•problem solving and decision making</td><td>Items 3–7
(written)</td><td>17–20</td><td>13–16</td><td>10–12</td><td>0–9</td></tr>
<tr><td>Items 8–12
(multiple-choice)</td><td>20</td><td>16</td><td>8–12</td><td>0–4</td></tr>
<tr><td>Part 3: Word Skills
•noun suffixes
•synonyms and antonyms
•multiple-meaning words
•syllables</td><td>Items 13–17</td><td>15</td><td>12</td><td>9</td><td>0–6</td></tr>
<tr><td rowspan="3">Part 4: Writing and Language
Writing Fluency

Proofreading
•the vowel sounds in shout and wall, final schwa + r sounds, final schwa + l sounds, homophones
•adjectives, comparative forms of adjectives

Writing Skills
•combining sentences: compound subjects and compound predicates</td><td>Item 18
Fluency</td><td>20</td><td>15</td><td>10</td><td>0–5</td></tr>
<tr><td>Item 19
Language</td><td>8–9</td><td>6–7</td><td>4–5</td><td>0–3</td></tr>
<tr><td>Items 20–21
Writing Skills</td><td>8</td><td></td><td>4</td><td>0</td></tr>
<tr><td>Part 5: Self-Assessment (optional)
•self-assessment/reflection
•developing preferences</td><td>Home Letter</td><td colspan="4">Scoring of Self-Assessment is not recommended. Evaluate answers for evidence of metacognitive growth.</td></tr>
</table>

Total Score ______________

☐ Excellent (90–100)
☐ Good (75–89)
☐ Satisfactory (60–74)
☐ Needs Improvement (0–59)

Additional Comments ________________________

____

____

Test taken independently ☐
Test taken with partial support ☐
Test taken with full support ☐

In Try to See It My Way you read about how seeing things from different points of view can lead to greater understanding.

Now you will read a story in which a grandfather and his grandson have an important conversation. Thomas, the grandson, is upset that his aunt has come to live with them.

You will also read about a young girl who hasn't seen her aunt for many years. She is annoyed because her aunt keeps sending her gifts she will never use.

There are questions to answer before, during, and after your reading. You may go back to the selections to help you answer the questions.

1 READING STRATEGIES

1. **Self-Question** Think about what you have read in the introduction. What are some reasons Thomas might be upset about his aunt?

____

____

____

____

____

from
Stealing Home

by Mary Stolz

She had made, in the time she'd been with them, lots of changes in their house, in their lives. Grandfather, trying to look on the sunny side, said it wasn't all bad, now was it, Thomas?

They were sitting on the front-porch swing, Ringo on his railing perch, listening to the evening choir of birds. Aunt Linzy had gone to visit Mrs. Price. They'd become vegetarian friends and exchanged recipes about how to make turnips exciting and amaze people with tofu. Or make soup from plums.

"Plum soup," Thomas said irritably. "That's crazy."

"Tasted pretty good, didn't it?"

Thomas wriggled. "I suppose."

"Do you want to talk about it, Thomas?"

"About what?"

"Now, now. You know about what."

"What's to say?"

"I know how difficult this is being for you. But don't you think it *could* be worse?"

"How?"

"Well—Ivan doesn't bite us anymore. There's that."

"Hah-hah."

After a short silence, Grandfather said, "Your aunt Linzy has a good disposition, which is nothing to hah-hah about. Too many people are constantly whining and complaining about their lot in life. You must admit your aunt is usually pretty cheerful."

"And I think it's funny."

"What do you mean?"

"Grandfather. If you lived someplace where people were wondering how much longer you were going to stay, would you be cheerful? I wouldn't be. I'd be—" He hesitated.

"What would you be?"

Grumpy, Thomas started to say, but changed his mind. "Sad, I guess."

"Thomas, tell me. Have you once tried to look at this situation from your aunt's point of view instead of your own?"

"No. Have you?"

"Yes. Could you try?"

"No."

Grandfather continued to have the waiting look he got when he expected something more from Thomas.

Stop here and answer Question 2. Then continue reading.

READING STRATEGIES (continued)

2. **Monitor** What does Grandfather seem to want from Thomas?

____

____

____

____

____

Rubric Score for Items 1–2 _______

8

"She took my room away from me."

"We're making out all right in mine, aren't we?"

"It isn't that, Grandfather—"

"I know." He held up one hand. "You needn't say what you're thinking. But *I* am thinking of what people all over the world have to endure that you and I do not. Millions of human beings hungry, hopeless, frightened. *Homeless,* Thomas. Nowhere to *live.* You and I just have to put up for a while with one lonely old lady."

"What does 'for a while' mean? I don't think it's for a while. I think she's *living* with us."

"Thomas, Thomas. You don't often disappoint me. But sometimes you do, really you do. If that should be the case—what do you suggest? Tell her to pack up and get out?"

"She stole my cat."

Thomas looked at Ringo, beautiful and composed on the railing. It made his throat, and his heart, really ache—the way Ringo had left him for Aunt Linzy.

Grandfather put an arm over Thomas's shoulders and pulled him close.

"Things never can remain the same, Thomas. It's the way life is. . . . Everything changes, and we can't stop that."

Thomas sighed. Grandfather always knew what he was thinking. "You don't bicker with her anymore, do you?"

"No. It would make things worse."

"I'm not being a good sport, am I?"

"Not especially."

"I don't want to disappoint you, Grandfather."

"I know that."

"I'll try to be better."

Thomas learned an important lesson. Now read about a young girl who tries to teach her aunt a lesson about sending "garbage gifts."

Garbage Gifts

from *Encore! More Winning Monologs for Young Actors*
by Peg Kehret

Last year, I thought I had figured out a way to educate Aunt Marie so she wouldn't keep wasting her money on gifts I'll never use. I bought a present for her, wrapped it, and had it ready to add to the box that Mom always sends to Aunt Marie for her birthday. I figured when Aunt Marie opened my present, it would make her think twice before she sent me something inappropriate.

When Mom started packing the box for Aunt Marie, she picked up my present, felt of it, and said, "It feels like a ping-pong paddle."

I said that's exactly what it was. Mom told me Aunt Marie is sixty-nine years old and will have no use for a ping-pong paddle. I said I didn't expect her to use it.

And that's when Mom told me about Aunt Marie's life. Aunt Marie lost her husband when she was thirty years old; he died in a fire which also gutted their home. Her only child, a son, was killed ten years later, in the war. Aunt Marie doesn't have much money and she probably goes without something she needs herself in order to remember all of us with gifts on our birthdays and at Christmas. She does it because we are the only family she has left.

"I know the things she sends you are too babyish," Mom said, "but she sends them out of love. And if you want to send something to Aunt Marie, it must be chosen with love, too."

I wondered what it would be like to have your only family be people you never see.

2 COMPREHENSION

Write your answers to these questions.

3. How does Thomas feel about his aunt moving in? Why does
    he feel this way?

4. How are Thomas's feelings about Aunt Linzy different from
    Grandfather's?

5. How does Grandfather try to help Thomas change his
    attitude?

6. What does Thomas mean when he says that Aunt Linzy stole his cat?

____

____

____

____

____

7. Do you think Thomas will change his mind about Aunt Linzy? Give clues from the story in your answer.

____

____

____

____

____

Rubric Score for Items 3–7 _______
20

8. How long does the story suggest Aunt Linzy will stay with Grandfather and Thomas?

    ○ a. for one more day
    ○ b. for a long time
    ○ c. until after supper
    ○ d. until Grandfather tells her to leave

9. What example does Grandfather use to show Thomas that things are not so bad for them?

    ○ a. The sun is shining.
    ○ b. Plum soup tastes good.
    ○ c. Too many people whine and complain.
    ○ d. Many people are homeless and hungry.

10. Why does Thomas say he will try to do better?

    ○ a. He decides he really does like Aunt Linzy.
    ○ b. He doesn't want to upset Grandfather.
    ○ c. He wants to be friends with Ringo again.
    ○ d. He thinks it will help him get his old room back.

11. Think about the children in each selection. How is Thomas's situation similar to that of Aunt Marie's niece?

    ○ a.   They are both thinking only of themselves.
    ○ b.   They both have aunts that live with them.
    ○ c.   They both enjoy getting gifts.
    ○ d.   They both feel sorry for their aunts.

12. What do you think Aunt Marie's niece will do with the ping-pong paddle?

    ○ a.   send it to Aunt Marie
    ○ b.   keep it for herself
    ○ c.   return it and buy some candy with the money
    ○ d.   exchange it for a more appropriate gift

Score for Items 8–12 (x4) _______
20

Read the sentence or sentences. Use what you know about figuring out new words to help you select the correct answer.

13. *Aunt Linzy had gone to visit Mrs. Price. They'd become vegetarian friends and <u>exchanged</u> recipes about how to make turnips exciting and amaze people with tofu.*

    What did they do with the recipes?
    - a.   cooked them
    - b.   traded them
    - c.   made new ones
    - d.   sold them

14. *"Plum soup," Thomas said <u>irritably</u>. "That's crazy."*

    Which choice shows *irritably* correctly divided into syllables?
    - a.   ir•ri•ta•bly
    - b.   irr•it•ably
    - c.   irr•i•tab•ly
    - d.   ir•rit•ably

15. *"Too many people are constantly whining and complaining about their <u>lot</u> in life."*

    What does Grandfather feel that too many people are unhappy with?
    - a.   their plot of land
    - b.   their lack of money
    - c.   what has happened to them
    - d.   their many belongings

16. *"You needn't say what you're thinking. But I am thinking
of what people all over the world have to <u>endure</u> that you
and I do not."*

What are people all over the world having
to do?
- ○ a.   put an end to things
- ○ b.   hear about unpleasant things
- ○ c.   put up with unpleasant things
- ○ d.   move in with relatives

17. *"Thomas, Thomas. You don't often <u>disappoint</u> me. But
sometimes you do, really you do."*

Grandfather is expressing his __________.
- ○ a.   disagreement
- ○ b.   disappointment
- ○ c.   disappointing
- ○ d.   disapprove

Score for Items 13–17 (x3) __________
15

18. Write one or two paragraphs about one of the topics below.

    a. If you could trade places with someone else for one week, whom would you choose and why? Write about what you think you would learn.

    b. Write about a time when you disagreed with someone. Explain the different points of view.

Rubric Score for Item 18 (x5) _______

20

19. Read the following post card. Find and correct nine errors.
Use what you know about proofreading to make your
corrections. The examples may help you. There are five
spelling errors and four errors in adjectives.

Dear Aunt Myrtle,

Greetings from Florida! Yesterday was the ~~more~~ most
exciting day of awl. We went fishing in the ocean.
Uncle Carl took us out on his boat. I road in the
bow of the boat with Katy.

After about a hour, I felt a tug on my line. You
should've heard me showt! I stayed calm, though,
and knew exactly what to do. I caught an huge
silvur fish all by myself. Katy caught a fish too,
aulthough hers was more smaller than mine. Uncle
Carl caught the most biggest fish I have ever seen!
It was a very speciel day. I'll write you again soon.

       Love,

       Lena

Mrs. Myrtle McGuane
346 Q St., N.W.
Washington, D.C. 20007

Score for Item 19 _______
        9

Choose the correct way to combine each pair of sentences into one sentence with either a compound subject or a compound predicate.

20. Lena went fishing with Uncle Carl.

    Katy went fishing with Uncle Carl.

    ○ a. Lena went fishing with Katy and Uncle Carl.
    ○ b. Lena and Katy went fishing with Uncle Carl.
    ○ c. Lena went fishing with Uncle Carl, and so did Katy.
    ○ d. Lena went fishing with Uncle Carl, and Katy went fishing with Uncle Carl.

21. Katy felt a tug on her line.

    Katy reeled in the fish.

    ○ a. Katy felt a tug on her line, Katy reeled in the fish.
    ○ b. Katy felt a tug on her line, reeled in the fish.
    ○ c. Katy felt a tug on her line and reeled in the fish.
    ○ d. Katy felt a tug on her line, and Katy reeled in the fish.

Score for Items 20–21 (x4) _______

8

5 HOME LETTER

Write a letter to a friend or relative. Your letter should show that you have thought about what you have read.

Date________________________

Dear ____________________________ ,

    We have just finished the theme called Try to See It My Way. It was about the different ways in which different people see things.

    In reading about other points of view, I learned ________________________

____

____

    My favorite story in this theme was ____________________________________

because ____

____

    My favorite character was ____

I especially liked this character because ___________________________________

____

____

    I wish ____________________ would see my point of view when we

disagree about ____

Sincerely,

____

CATASTROPHE!

LEVEL 5, THEME 4

Integrated Theme Test Record

Student ____ Date ____________

STUDENT PROFILE					
Part Scores:	Excellent Progress	Good Progress	Some Progress	Needs Improvement
Part 1: Reading Strategies •self-question •monitor	Items 1–2	7–8	5–6	3–4	0–2
Part 2: Comprehension •cause and effect •making generalizations •drawing conclusions	Items 3–7 (written)	17–20	13–16	10–12	0–9
	Items 8–12 (multiple-choice)	20	16	8–12	0–4
Part 3: Word Skills •analogies •word roots •compound words	Items 13–17	15	12	9	0–6
Part 4: Writing and Language Writing Fluency	Item 18 Fluency	20	15	10	0–5
Proofreading •compound words, the VCV, VCCV, and VCCCV patterns •verb tenses with past tense forms, subject-verb agreement, irregular verbs	Item 19 Language	8–9	6–7	4–5	0–3
Writing Skills •paraphrasing	Item 20 Writing Skills	8	6	4	0–2
Part 5: Self-Assessment (optional) •self-assessment/reflection •developing preferences	Magazine Interview	Scoring of Self-Assessment is not recommended. Evaluate answers for evidence of metacognitive growth.			

Total Score

____

- ☐ Excellent (90–100)
- ☐ Good (75–89)
- ☐ Satisfactory (60–74)
- ☐ Needs Improvement (0–59)

Additional Comments ___________________________

____

____

____

Test taken independently ☐

Test taken with partial support ☐

Test taken with full support ☐

Name ____

In Catastrophe! you read about disasters and about ways that people have coped with them.

Now you will read about the deadliest natural disaster in United States history, a hurricane that hit Galveston, Texas, in 1900, and about weatherman Dr. Isaac Cline's heroic efforts to save the people of his town. You will also read a fictional passage about another Galveston hurricane.

There are questions to answer before, during, and after your reading. You may go back to the selections to help you answer the questions.

1 READING STRATEGIES

1. **Self-Question** Preview the article called "The Great Galveston Hurricane" by looking at the title and the pictures. Write a question that you think will be answered as you read.

____

____

____

____

____

THE GREAT GALVESTON HURRICANE

from *Hurricanes*
by Dennis Brindell Fradin

Early on the morning of September 8, the outskirts of the hurricane moved into Galveston. Gray, heavy clouds filled the sky. Rain fell. Dr. Cline knew that the winds of the hurricane were likely to push huge waves into Galveston. He got into a horse-drawn wagon and went along Galveston's beaches. "Move to higher ground!" he told people. Cline knew that the highest ground on the whole island was only nine feet above sea level. But that was better than the beach.

Few people left their homes for higher ground. Even those who expected a flood thought their homes could survive it.

The wind speed rose from 30 to 70 miles per hour on that terrible Saturday. When the gusts reached 120 miles per hour, the wind gauge was blown off the Weather Bureau building. Trees snapped. Telephone and telegraph lines went down. Roof tiles flew through the air like deadly hatchets. Soon the bridges leading out of Galveston were wrecked. The city was completely cut off from the rest of the world.

Stop **Stop here and answer Question 2. Then continue reading.**

The fury of the 1900 hurricane flung ships from the Galveston harbor.

READING STRATEGIES (continued)

2. Monitor What clues help you know this happened a long time ago?

____

____

____

____

____

Rubric Score for Items 1–2 _______

8

Then came the worst part. As people looked out their windows, they saw rising water moving over the beaches and on into the city. The water rushed into living rooms and sent people running up stairs. Even up high the screaming and crying people weren't safe. Smashed repeatedly by the waves, houses broke loose from the ground and swirled away.

Many people inside the houses were drowned. Some jumped out windows and swam for their lives. They grasped for trees, rooftops, and other floating debris.

Weatherman Isaac Cline watched the water rise higher and higher against his own house. Cline had built the house to resist hurricanes.

Knowing this, about fifty neighbors had come there for shelter. Houses near Cline's were smashed by the waves. The wreckage crashed against the Cline house. Finally, it, too, collapsed into the water.

Cline's pregnant wife and about thirty other people were drowned. But Dr. Cline and his daughter escaped the house through a hole in the roof. Two other Cline children jumped out a window and took refuge with their father on the floating roof.

There were many other amazing survival stories. One girl, Anna Delz, was flung into the water when her house collapsed. Anna grabbed a tree and floated with it for a while. Then she grabbed onto a roof that came floating along. When the roof began to crumble, she held onto a big piece of wood. Mile after mile she floated. Anna Delz was carried to safety eighteen miles from Galveston.

The waves were so powerful that ships were flung from Galveston's harbor. One, the *Taunton,* was thrown onto the Texas mainland in Chambers County, twenty-two miles from Galveston.

Late on the evening of September 8, the hurricane moved out of Galveston. As the water went down, the stunned survivors saw thousands of bodies in the muck. A total of at least 7,200 people lay dead in and around Galveston. That is the highest death toll the United States has ever had in a natural disaster.

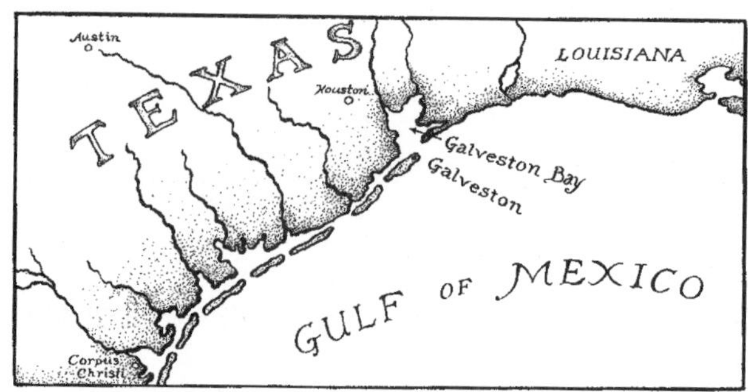

A train nearly topples from the force of the water during the 1900 hurricane.

Now read a fictional account of another hurricane in Galveston. This one happened more recently.

FROM THE SILENT STORM

by Sherry Garland

"Let's hold hands," Ty suggested as he caught his breath. Alyssa took one hand and Dylan took the other. All of their hands were slippery, making it difficult to hang on. The wind pushed their backs like an angry bully forcing them to trot to keep from being shoved to the ground. Although they were tired and out of breath, they had no choice but to keep moving.

Along the road, summerhouses creaked on their stilts and shingles flipped off. A few of the poorly built houses, or ones still under construction, had given in to the wind already. Plywood flapped where nails had not been hammered in well, and small trees planted in the spring rolled across the yards. Boats that hadn't been properly secured—mostly those of people who lived far away—had flipped over onto their sides in driveways or slid across the road into the marshes. The electric company had already cut off the electricity to prevent fires and electrocutions, sinking the island in eerie darkness. As far as Alyssa could tell, nearly everyone on the west end had evacuated for higher ground. The three long-horn cattle she had seen being loaded into trailers were gone.

The closer they came to the ocean, the deeper the water. At last they saw Captain Mac's stables. With a burst of energy, they dashed to the low wood building and ducked inside. It was empty.

"Where are all the horses?" Ty asked as he leaned against a stall door, catching his breath. Waist-deep water covered the sandy floor. Brushes and pieces of tack floated about, bumping against the stalls. A couple of dead fish had lodged in the hay. Outside, the waves beat continuously against the walls.

"Are we going to stay here?" Dylan asked, then collapsed on top of the metal feed bin. He pressed his back against a bale of hay. "I'm too tired to go any farther."

Write your answers to these questions.

3. Why should people move to higher ground during
    a hurricane?

    ____

    ____

    ____

    ____

    ____

4. Do you think most of the people living on Galveston Island
    had ever experienced a hurricane? Why or why not? Give
    clues from the selection in your answer.

    ____

    ____

    ____

    ____

5. Why did Dr. Cline's house collapse even though it was built
    to resist hurricanes?

    ____

    ____

    ____

    ____

    ____

6. What two things make hurricanes dangerous? Tell why.

What	Why

7. Why is the 1900 Galveston hurricane called the deadliest natural disaster in United States history?

____

____

____

____

____

Rubric Score for Items 3–7 _______

20

Choose the best answer and fill in the circle.

8. What is one way a city like Galveston could become "cut off from the rest of the world" during a hurricane?

   ○ a. Shifting sand dunes could bury the city.
   ○ b. All of the people could be drowned.
   ○ c. Telephone lines could be torn down.
   ○ d. The city could be lifted away from the earth by the wind.

9. How were some people able to survive?

   ○ a. They held on to floating objects.
   ○ b. They rode horses out of town.
   ○ c. They hid in their stables.
   ○ d. They rode in boats to the mainland.

10. Which of the following is probably true?

   ○ a. Winds always cause the most damage in a hurricane.
   ○ b. It is impossible to protect yourself against a hurricane.
   ○ c. Hurricane winds can move large objects.
   ○ d. Water levels in a hurricane rise slowly.

11. What would be a good thing for Alyssa, Dylan, and Ty to do?

    ○ a. stay in the stables
    ○ b. get to higher ground
    ○ c. take a nap
    ○ d. look for Captain Mac

12. Which of these is true of Galveston?

    ○ a. Its population is 7200.
    ○ b. It was not rebuilt after the 1900 hurricane.
    ○ c. It no longer has telephone service.
    ○ d. It is a low-lying island.

Score for Items 8–12 (x4) _______
20

3 WORD SKILLS

Read the sentence or sentences. Use what you know about figuring out new words to help you select the correct answer.

13. *Early on the morning of September 8, the* <u>outskirts</u> *of the hurricane moved into Galveston.*

    What part of the storm moved into Galveston that morning?
    - ○ a.   the center of the storm
    - ○ b.   the edges of the storm
    - ○ c.   news about the storm
    - ○ d.   the worst part of the storm

14. *Few people left their homes for higher ground. Even those who expected a flood thought their homes could survive it.*

    Complete this analogy: <u>High ground</u> is to <u>sea level</u> as <u>survive</u> is to ____________.
    - ○ a.   flood
    - ○ b.   resist
    - ○ c.   collapse
    - ○ d.   homes

15. *The waves were so powerful that ships were flung from Galveston's harbor. One, the* Taunton, *was thrown onto the Texas* <u>mainland</u> *in Chambers County, twenty-two miles from Galveston.*

    Where was the *Taunton* found after the hurricane?
    - ○ a.   on the major land area of Texas
    - ○ b.   on a nearby island
    - ○ c.   in Galveston's harbor
    - ○ d.   twenty-two miles from Texas

16. *Cline had built the house to resist hurricanes. Knowing
    this, about fifty neighbors had come there for shelter.*

    Complete this analogy: House is to shelter as hurricane is
    to __________ .
    - ○ a.   wind
    - ○ b.   flood
    - ○ c.   storm
    - ○ d.   rain

17. *A few of the poorly built houses, or ones still under
    construction, had given in to the wind already.*

    What types of houses are houses under
    construction?
    - ○ a.   houses that are built to resist hurricanes
    - ○ b.   houses in the process of being built
    - ○ c.   houses that were built last year
    - ○ d.   houses that are in the process of being torn apart

Score for Items 13–17 (x3) __________
15

18. Write one or two paragraphs about one of the topics below.

   a. While walking home from school, you notice that a neighbor's house is on fire. Tell what you would do and why.

   b. Have you survived a catastrophe, or do you know someone who has? Write about your own, or someone else's, experience in a disaster.

Rubric Score for Item 18 (x5) _______

20

19. Read the following review by a television movie critic. Find and correct nine errors. Use what you know about proofreading to make your corrections. The examples may help you. There are four spelling errors and five verb errors.

Channel 24 Movie Review

Hello, movie fans. Well, this summer's big disaster film, *Mudslide,*
finally open_^ yesterday. Take it from me, everything about the movie is

a catastrophe. I could barely control my disgust while I watched it. It

oozes bad acting, bad camera work, and bad special effects. The story

have the same old elements: a mysterious stranger, citizens who don't

seem to nottice a mountain of mud coming their way, and only one

sane person, whom no-body listen to.

These are the same folks who bringed us *Haunted Hallway* and

Attack of the Flying Fish, which I reviewd on this program last year.

It were a struggle to sit through the enttire movie, but somehow I

muddled through. Only one word can experess how I feel about

Mudslide: Yuck!

Score for Item 19 ________
9

20. Now write a paragraph that paraphrases, or restates, the movie review
on the previous page. Remember to include only the important ideas.

____

____

____

____

____

____

____

____

____

____

Rubric Score for Item 20 (x2) _______
8

5 MAGAZINE INTERVIEW

You have been chosen to do an interview with a
new students' magazine. Answer the interview questions
below. There are no right or wrong answers, but your answers
should show that you have thought about what you have read.

Students Read About Catastrophes

Students at the _____________________ School have been learning about
all kinds of disasters. *Students Want to Know* sent an editor to interview
one of the students, _____________________ , about the experience.

Editor: What did you learn about disasters while reading Catastrophe?

Student: ____

____

Editor: Which selection did you find most interesting? What about the

selection made it stand out in your mind?

Student: ____

____

____

____

Editor: How have you become a better reader since reading this theme?

Student: ____

____

____

Editor: What topics from this theme would you like to learn more about?

Student: ____

____

FROM THE PRAIRIE TO THE SEA

LEVEL 5, THEME 5

Integrated Theme Test Record

Student ____ Date __________

STUDENT PROFILE					
	Part Scores:	Excellent Progress	Good Progress	Some Progress	Needs Improvement
Part 1: Reading Strategies •self-question •summarize	Items 1–2	7–8	5–6	3–4	0–2
Part 2: Comprehension •propaganda •making judgments •following directions	Items 3–7 (written)	17–20	13–16	10–12	0–9
	Items 8–12 (multiple-choice)	20	16	8–12	0–4
Part 3: Word Skills •word roots •prefixes •contractions and possessives	Items 13–17	15	12	9	0–6
Part 4: Writing and Language Writing Fluency	Item 18 Fluency	20	15	10	0–5
Proofreading •adding -ed or -ing, changing final y to i, adding -ion •punctuating dialogue, subject/object pronouns, possessive pronouns, and contractions with pronouns	Item 19 Language	8–9	6–7	4–5	0–3
Writing Skills •answering an essay question	Item 20 Writing Skills	8		4	0
Part 5: Self-Assessment (optional) •self-assessment/reflection •developing preferences	Poster	Scoring of Self-Assessment is not recommended. Evaluate answers for evidence of metacognitive growth.			

Total Score _______________

☐ Excellent (90–100)
☐ Good (75–89)
☐ Satisfactory (60–74)
☐ Needs Improvement (0–59)

Additional Comments _______________________

____

____

____

Test taken independently ☐

Test taken with partial support ☐

Test taken with full support ☐

In the theme From the Prairie to the Sea, you read about life in the Old West. Now you will read a passage about some things that were important to a cowboy in the West. You will also read a passage that describes the Spanish influence on American cowboys.

There are questions to answer before, during, and after your reading. You may go back to the selections to help you answer the questions.

1   READING STRATEGIES

1. **Self-Question** Preview the two selections by looking at each title and all of the pictures. Write a question that you think will be answered as you read.

____

____

____

____

____

from Cowboys of the Wild West

by Russell Freedman

The lariat was an essential tool during roundups, brandings, and cattle drives. Made of tough, twisted plant fiber or braided rawhide, it could be anywhere from thirty to sixty feet long. With practice, almost anyone could learn to throw a lariat while standing on the ground. But it took considerable skill to do the same thing from the back of a galloping horse that was chasing a twisting, dodging steer.

A cowboy's saddle was another essential piece of equipment. Since he spent most of his waking hours in his saddle, it had to be comfortable. And it had to be ruggedly built to withstand plenty of hard wear. Strangers could judge a man's standing in the cowboy trade by the make and condition of his saddle. If it was built well and maintained with care, a cowboy could ride for hours without making his horse uncomfortable or sore.

A saddle weighed between thirty and forty pounds. It was made from a carved wooden frame covered with leather. At the front of the saddle was a horn, used to secure the lariat when the cowboy roped a steer. The cowboy's legs hung down over leather flaps called "fenders." His boots rested on broad wooden or metal stirrups. He could stand in the stirrups while riding down a steep slope or trotting along the trail. The "cinch" went around the horse's body and under its belly, holding the saddle in place. Long leather ties were used to attach bedrolls, rain slickers, and other gear.

A fine saddle, handmade by a master craftsman in a western town, could cost more than a month's pay. A cowboy might be willing to risk losing his custom-made boots, his silver spurs, or his best Stetson on the outcome of a horse race or some other sporting event, but he would part with his saddle only in the most desperate circumstances. To say of a cowboy, "He's sold his saddle," meant that he was quitting the cowboy trade for good.

Stop here and answer Question 2. Then continue reading.

READING STRATEGIES (continued)

2. **Summarize** Why is a cowboy's saddle important to him? Give two reasons.

____

____

____

____

____

____

Rubric Score for Items 1–2 _______

8

Every cowboy owned his saddle, but he did not always own a horse. Horses were furnished by the ranch or trail outfit he was working for. If he had a horse, he kept it with the ranch's common pool of horses as long as he was employed there. Usually, he was given the use of perhaps six or eight horses by the rancher or trail boss who hired him. Saddle horses were ridden hard, and a man might change mounts several times a day. As long as a cowboy stayed with an outfit, the string of horses assigned to him were his, as surely as if he did own them. If a boss wanted a man to quit, he would take the cowboy's favorite horse away from him. That always meant that the cowboy should leave of his own accord before he had to be fired.

Most of these horses were mustang ponies, which ran wild on the western plains. A hardy breed—small, tough, and fast—they were captured and tamed by both the Plains Indians and by white settlers in the West. Cowboys preferred them to the larger horses imported from the East. "Beautiful little creatures they were—generally cream, buckskin, or mouse-colored," recalled a Texas cowboy named James Cook. "As a rule they were clean-limbed, and their hoofs were black and perfect. No blacksmith or hoof-shaper had ever tinkered with their feet or forced them to wear iron shoes, and their hoofs would stand wear over the roughest trails. They required no grain, but rustled food for themselves."

Mustangs came from open rangeland, where they roamed free until about the age of four. Every spring, these four-year-olds were captured, driven to corrals, then tamed to the saddle and trained. Taming was called "breaking" or "busting," which meant that the animal's wild spirit was literally "broken" as the horse learned to fear, respect, and obey its rider. A broncobuster might be any local cowboy who was a good rider, or he might be a professional buster who traveled from ranch to ranch.

There was no easy way to break a wild bronco that had never been ridden before. The struggling horse was roped, tied to a post, and bridled. After the bridle came the saddle blanket, the saddle, and then the rider. With his spurs, his quirt (a short whip), and his rope end, the broncobuster beat in the lesson that disobedience brings instant

punishment. No matter how violently the horse kicked and bucked, the buster would break its spirit and ride it to a standstill.

Once broken, the horse was trained to help its rider handle cattle. A clever horse was said to have "cow sense." Horses with special talents or abilities were favored for certain jobs. A good distance horse had long legs, lots of endurance, and an easy gait. A horse used for night herding had to have keen eyesight, a sure sense of direction, and a calm disposition.

"On warm moonlit nights as I rode around the herd, I would say to myself, 'This is the life!'" James Cook remembered. "My horse seemed to understand my thoughts, and to share my feeling. I always picked the best horse in my string for my night animal, and used him whenever I had to night herd. He and I became real friends. When I was in a merry mood he seemed to feel the same way, and on dark and stormy nights when the cattle were ready to jump and stampede at any minute and everyone was keyed up, I could feel him trembling under me; occasionally when we stood still, I could hear his heart thumping with excitement."

THE AMERICAN COWBOY

from *Kids Discover* magazine

In the 16th century, Spaniards trained Native Americans and later poor Mexicans to be vaqueros, *or cowhands. These poor ranch workers invented new ways to rope, ride, and drive cattle. Later, cowpunchers in California, Texas, and other places picked up these skills, along with the Spanish words that went with them.*

In 1493, Columbus brought horses and cattle to a land that had neither. The animals roamed freely on the fenceless wilderness. So, from time to time, someone had to go get them. That, in a nutshell, is the job of a cowboy.

These early cow handlers had a Spanish name: *vaqueros,* from *vaca* (cow). Over a period of four centuries, horses, cattle, and the folks who tended them spread south to Argentina and north to Canada. But it was in the western United States that the lifestyle of simple, hardworking ranch hands grew into legend.

Americans turned the word *vaqueros* into buckaroos. In time, many other colorful names evolved, such as cowpunchers, wranglers, and saddle slickers. But mostly, people called them cowgirls and cowboys.

Their heyday was between the American Civil War (1861–65) and the turn of the century (1900). But real cowfolk are still around. And so are their legends in books, movies, and songs.

The Well-fitted Cowboy

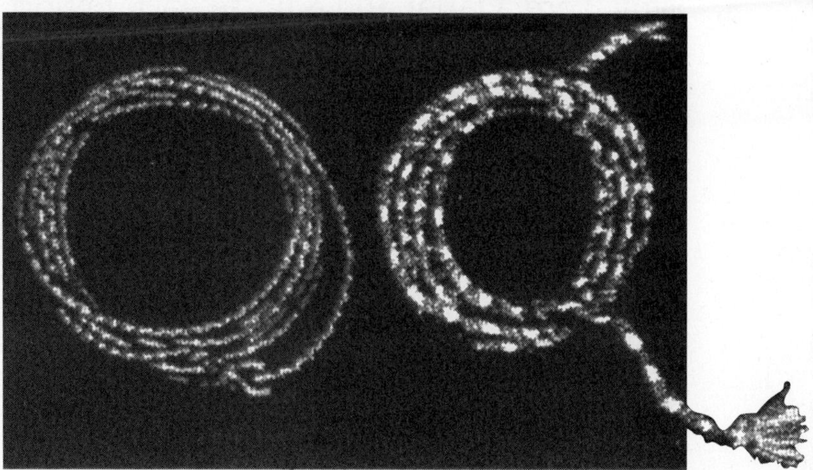

In Spanish, la riata *(la ree AH ta), means "the rope." Say it fast. Faster. Soon, you'll say it cowboy-style: lariat. A lariat, or lasso, is a long rope with a loop for catching cattle and horses.*

Early Spanish Vaquero. Wide-brimmed, low-crowned sombrero. Leggings. Short pants and jacket. Big spurs.

Mexican Vaquero. Very large, ornamented sombrero. Tight, buttoned leather chaps. Large heel spurs.

2 COMPREHENSION

Write your answers to these questions.

3. Why were a lariat and a horse each important things
   for a cowboy?

   ____

   ____

   ____

   ____

4. Based on what you have read, do you think it was better for a
   cowboy to use the ranch horses or to use his own? Explain why.

   ____

   ____

   ____

   ____

   ____

5. What were the steps in taming a wild bronco? List them in
   order in the chart.

   1. First, you must rope the horse.

   2. ____

   3. ____

   4. ____

   5. ____

   6. Finally, ride the horse to a standstill.

6. Reread the last paragraph of "Cowboys of the Wild West."
    How does James Cook feel about cowboy life? Why does he
    feel this way?

    ____

    ____

    ____

    ____

    ____

7. According to the selection, *Strangers could judge a man's
    standing in the cowboy trade by the make and condition of
    his saddle.*

    What specific things could a stranger learn about a cowboy
    from the condition of his saddle?

    ____

    ____

    ____

    ____

    ____

Rubric Score for Items 3–7 ________
                                20

Choose the best answer and fill in the circle.

8. Why did cowboys prefer mustangs over other types
   of horses?

   - ○ a. Mustangs could control other horses because of
     their large size.
   - ○ b. Mustangs were quick and strong.
   - ○ c. Mustangs were easy to tame.
   - ○ d. Mustangs were naturally gentle and obedient.

9. According to "The American Cowboy," who developed
   most of the skills and styles we associate with
   cowboys today?

   - ○ a. Christopher Columbus
   - ○ b. Spanish horse and cattle importers
   - ○ c. Native Americans and Mexicans hired by the Spanish
   - ○ d. the stars of cowboy movies

10. Why would a cowboy consider his saddle more important
    than boots, spurs, or a Stetson hat?

    - ○ a. He could not do his job without one.
    - ○ b. A saddle was very expensive.
    - ○ c. A saddle had the owner's name on it.
    - ○ d. A saddle was handed down from father to son.

11. What step would a broncobuster take if a horse resisted
being ridden?

    ○ a. He would ride the horse until it obeyed.
    ○ b. He would get rid of the horse and find another one.
    ○ c. He would turn it over to a more experienced broncobuster.
    ○ d. He would give the horse a job that did not require
        it to be ridden.

12. Suppose you wanted to sell a horse to a cowboy.
What could you say to persuade him it was a good horse?

    ○ a. This is the wildest, meanest horse you can find.
    ○ b. This horse was very devoted to its previous owner.
    ○ c. This horse does not have to be fed; it finds its own
        grain.
    ○ d. This horse is strong and easygoing.

Score for Items 8–12 (x4) ________
                                                            20

3 WORD SKILLS

Read the sentence or sentences. Use what you know about figuring out new words to help you select the correct answer.

13. *Cowboys preferred mustangs to the larger horses <u>imported</u> from the East.*

    What does this sentence tell you about the larger horses?
    - a. They were important in the East but not in the West.
    - b. They were bought at ports in the East.
    - c. They were sent from the East to the West.
    - d. They were too big to do the kind of work the cowboys required.

14. *Taming was called "breaking" or "busting," which meant that the animal's wild spirit was literally "broken" as the horse learned to fear, <u>respect</u>, and obey its rider.*

    Why was it important that a horse respect its rider?
    - a. A horse that looked up to its rider was more willing to obey orders.
    - b. A rider wanted a horse to feel responsible for the cattle.
    - c. Cowboys wanted to be liked by their horses.
    - d. A rider wanted a horse that could make its own decisions.

15. *With his spurs, his quirt (a short whip), and his rope end, the broncobuster beat in the lesson that <u>disobedience</u> brings instant punishment.*

    A broncobuster was quick to punish a horse that ___________
    - a. obeyed without thinking.
    - b. was too slow to obey.
    - c. made a mistake.
    - d. did not obey him.

16. *To say of a cowboy, "He's sold his saddle," meant that he
was quitting the cowboy trade for good.*

In this sentence, which of the following means the same
as *He's*?
○ a. He was
○ b. He has
○ c. His
○ d. He is

17. *The lariat was an essential tool during roundups,
brandings, and cattle drives.*

What would happen if a cowboy did not have a lariat at
those events?
○ a. He would have to work harder to get the job done.
○ b. He would have to use a different tool.
○ c. He would be admired for working without a lariat.
○ d. He would not be able to take part in the events.

Score for Items 13–17 (x3) _______
15

4 WRITING AND LANGUAGE

18. Write one or two paragraphs about one of the topics below.

    a. What do you think was the best part about being a cowboy in the Old West? What was the worst part? Give reasons for your choices.

    b. Think of an occupation today that you consider both exciting and difficult. Tell what it would be like to have that job.

Rubric Score for Item 18 (x5) _______

20

19. Read the following passage. Find and correct nine errors.
Use what you know about proofreading to make your
corrections in the passage. The examples may help you.
There are three spelling errors and six errors in
punctuation and pronouns.

When ~~mine~~ ^{my} great-grandfather was twenty-three, he became a cook

for cowboys who drove cattle north out of Texas. "I was not happy with

my life," he explained, "so I decided to try a different direc_∧ion."

It took a lot of planing to create three hot meals a day for men on

a cattle drive. The chuck wagon was equiped for a journey that lasted

several months. It's drawers and cubbyholes held coffee, sugar, bacon,

beans, flour, salt, and other supplys. The cook also had to take care of

his wagon and the mules that pulled it. If the cowboys got sick, they

went to him as they're doctor.

To you or I, the job might seem exciting. My great-grandfather he

said it was the hardest work he ever did. "The hours were long, and the

conditions were tough, he said. "I wouldn't try it again.

Score for Item 19 _______
9

20. Write an answer to one of these essay questions.

   a. Suppose a family today is about to move from the
      eastern part of the United States to the West. How
      would their move be different from a similar move in
      pioneer times?

   b. Think of movies you have seen or stories you have read
      about cowboys. Based on what you have read in this
      theme, do you think they give an accurate or an
      inaccurate picture of cowboy life? Give some reasons.

Rubric Score for Item 20 (x2) ________

8

5 TRAIL MARKERS

Complete the following markers along a
western trail. Your answers should show that you have
thought about what you have read.

My favorite story in this theme

was ______________________________

because ______________________________

____

____

____

In reading the theme, I learned

____

____

____

____

____

____

Some new words I learned are

____

____

____

____

____

I want to learn more about

____

____

____

____

____

DO YOU BELIEVE THIS??

LEVEL 5, THEME 6

Integrated Theme Test Record

Student ___________________________________ Date ___________

STUDENT PROFILE					
	Part Scores:	Excellent Progress	Good Progress	Some Progress	Needs Improvement
Part 1: Reading Strategies •predict/infer •monitor	Items 1–2	7–8	5–6	3–4	0–2
Part 2: Comprehension •story structure and summarizing •noting details •fantasy and realism •topic, main idea, supporting details, and summarizing	Items 3–7 (written)	17–20	13–16	10–12	0–9
	Items 8–12 (multiple-choice)	20	16	8–12	0–4
Part 3: Word Skills •prefixes •word roots •using context	Items 13–17	15	12	9	0–6
Part 4: Writing and Language Writing Fluency	Item 18 Fluency	20	15	10	0–5
Proofreading •prefix *un-*, words with suffixes •adverbs, comparing with adverbs, double negatives, prepositional phrases; object pronouns in prepositional phrases, using *I* and *me*	Item 19 Language	8–9	6–7	4–5	0–3
Writing Skills •writing clearly with pronouns	Items 20–21 Writing Skills	8		4	0
Part 5: Self-Assessment (optional) •self-assessment/reflection •developing preferences	Newspaper Report	Scoring of Self-Assessment is not recommended. Evaluate answers for evidence of metacognitive growth.			

Total Score

____

- ☐ Excellent (90–100)
- ☐ Good (75–89)
- ☐ Satisfactory (60–74)
- ☐ Needs Improvement (0–59)

Additional Comments _______________________

____

Test taken independently ☐

Test taken with partial support ☐

Test taken with full support ☐

Name ____

Do You Believe This??

In Do You *Believe* This?? you read about incredible events that have occurred in real life and in the imaginations of writers.

Now you will read about a small creature named Stuart Little who is setting out on an important journey. You will also read a passage about E. B. White, the author who created Stuart.

There are questions to answer during and after your reading. You may go back to the selections to help you answer the questions.

The Elephant Hotel, near Atlantic City, NJ.

Upside-Down House, in Sunrise Village, FL.

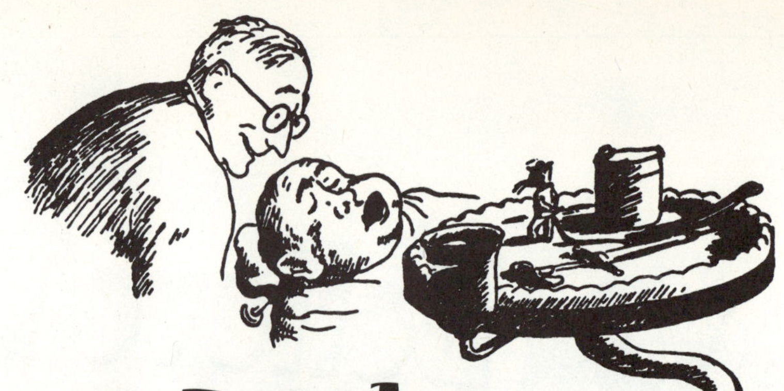

from

Stuart Little

by E. B. White

Stuart Little looks a lot like a mouse. He has decided to run away from home to search for a lost friend and to seek his fortune. Standing in the street in front of his house, Stuart realizes that he needs advice before he begins his journey. He decides to visit his friend Dr. Carey.

1 READING STRATEGIES

1. **Predict/Infer** What do you think Stuart will talk about with Dr. Carey?

____

____

____

____

"**T**ell me this, Stuart," said Dr. Carey. "How are you traveling? On foot?"

"Yes, sir," said Stuart.

"Well, I think you'd better have a car. As soon as I get this tooth out, we'll see what can be done about it. Open, please, Mr. Clydesdale."

Dr. Carey grabbed the tooth with the pincers again, and this time he pulled so long and so hard and with such determination that the tooth popped out, which was a great relief to everybody, particularly to Mr. Clydesdale. The Doctor then led Stuart into another room.

From a shelf he took a tiny automobile, about six inches long — the most perfect miniature automobile Stuart had ever seen. It was bright yellow with black fenders, a streamlined car of graceful design. "I made this myself," Dr. Carey said. "I enjoy building model cars and boats and other things when I am not extracting teeth. This car has a real gasoline motor in it. It has quite a good deal of power — do you think you can handle it, Stuart?"

"Certainly," replied Stuart, looking into the driver's seat and blowing the horn. "But isn't it going to attract too much attention? Won't everybody stop and stare at such a small automobile?"

"They would if they could see you," replied Dr. Carey, "but nobody will be able to see you, or the car."

"Why not?" asked Stuart.

"Because this automobile is a thoroughly modern car. It's not only noiseless, it's invisible. Nobody can see it."

Stop here and answer Question 2. Then continue reading.

READING STRATEGIES (continued)

2. **Monitor** What did Stuart and Dr. Carey talk about?

Rubric Score for Items 1–2 _______

8

"*I* can see it," remarked Stuart.

"Push that little button!" said the Doctor, pointing to a button on the instrument panel. Stuart pushed the button. Instantly the car vanished from sight.

"Now push it again," said the Doctor.

"How can I push it when I can't see it?" asked Stuart.

"Feel around for it."

So Stuart felt around until his hand came in contact with a button. It seemed like the same button, and Stuart pushed it. He heard a slight grinding noise and felt something slip out from under his hand.

"Hey, watch out!" yelled Dr. Carey. "You pushed the starter button. She's off! There she goes! She's away! She's loose in the room—now we'll never catch her." He grabbed Stuart up and placed him on a table where he wouldn't be hit by a runaway car.

"Oh, mercy! Oh, mercy!" Stuart cried when he realized what he had done. It was a very awkward situation. Neither Dr. Carey nor Stuart could see the little automobile, yet it was rushing all over the room under its own power, bumping into things. First there came a crashing noise over by the fireplace. The hearth broom fell down. Dr. Carey leapt for the spot and pounced on the place where the sound had come from. But though he was quick, he had hardly got his hands on the place when there was another crash over by the wastebasket. The Doctor pounced again. Pounce! Crash! Pounce! Crash! The Doctor was racing all over the room, pouncing and missing. It is almost impossible to catch a speedy invisible model automobile even when one is a skillful dentist.

"Oh, oh," yelled Stuart, jumping up and down. "I'm sorry, Dr. Carey, I'm dreadfully sorry!"

"Get a butterfly net!" shouted the Doctor.

"I can't," said Stuart. "I'm not big enough to carry a butterfly net."

"That's true," said Dr. Carey. "I forgot. My apologies, Stuart."

"The car is bound to stop sometime," said Stuart, "because it will run out of gas."

"That's true, too," said the Doctor. And so he and Stuart sat down and waited patiently until they no longer heard any crashing sounds in the room. Then the Doctor got down on his hands and knees and crawled cautiously all over, feeling here and there, until at last he found the car. It was in the fireplace, buried up to its hubs in wood ashes. The Doctor pressed the proper button and there it stood in plain sight again, its front fenders crumpled, its radiator leaking, its headlights broken, its windshield shattered, its right rear tire punctured, and quite a bit of yellow paint scratched off the hood.

"What a mess!" groaned the Doctor. "Stuart, I hope this will be a lesson to you: never push a button on an automobile unless you are sure of what you are doing."

"Yes, sir," answered Stuart, and his eyes filled with tears, each tear being smaller than a drop of dew.

You might think that writers get their ideas automatically. Actually, it takes time and work. Read the article below to see how E. B. White got his ideas for *Stuart Little*.

from

E. B. White: Some Writer!

by Beverly Gherman

In the spring of 1939 Andy [E. B. White] had sent his editor some pages he had been working on for a children's story about Stuart Little, a tiny creature wearing a hat and twirling a cane, who had come to him in a dream twelve years earlier. Over the years he had been telling Stuart stories to all his nieces and nephews, and once Joel [E. B. White's son] was old enough, he began telling them to Joel. He was not good at making them up on the spot. Instead he wrote down his ideas whenever they occurred to him.

Only recently had he thought they might become a book. But he was not rushing it. "I would rather wait a year than publish a bad children's book," he told his editor, "as I have too much respect for children."

2 COMPREHENSION

Write your answers to these questions.

3. Why does Stuart think Dr. Carey's car is perfect?

____

____

____

4. List one detail for Stuart, Dr. Carey, and the car that helps
you know that the story is a fantasy. Fill in the chart below.

Stuart
Dr. Carey
the car

5. What happened to cause a problem for Stuart and
Dr. Carey?

____

____

____

6. Give two reasons why Stuart begins to cry when he sees the
wrecked car.

____

____

____

____

7. Why did E. B. White wait a long time to publish his story
about Stuart Little?

____

____

____

____

Rubric Score for Items 3–7 _______
20

Choose the best answer and fill in the circle.

8. Why does Stuart push the wrong button on
   the car?

   ○ a.   He wants to play a trick on Dr. Casey.
   ○ b.   He can't see the button.
   ○ c.   He wants to see how fast the car will go.
   ○ d.   The car is going too fast.

9. What was Stuart doing while Dr. Carey was searching
   for the car?

   ○ a.   driving the car
   ○ b.   holding the butterfly net
   ○ c.   hiding
   ○ d.   standing on top of a table

10. Why does the car finally stop?

   ○ a.   Stuart jumps in and hits the brakes.
   ○ b.   The car runs out of gas.
   ○ c.   Dr. Casey catches it.
   ○ d.   It smashes into the fireplace.

11. What is the best way to summarize the end of the first selection?

○ a.   Stuart drove away in his new car.
○ b.   Dr. Casey found the car in the fireplace.
○ c.   Dr. Casey found the damaged car and Stuart felt bad.
○ d.   Stuart and Dr. Casey fixed the damaged model.

12. What helped E. B. White write *Stuart Little*?

○ a.   He used notes from stories that he'd told.
○ b.   He had a friend who was small and looked like a mouse.
○ c.   He got advice from Dr. Carey.
○ d.   His son Joel gave him ideas.

Score for Items 8–12 (x4) _______
20

3 WORD SKILLS

Read the sentence or sentences. Use what you know about figuring out new words to help you select the correct answer.

13. *From a shelf he took a tiny automobile, about six inches long—the most perfect <u>miniature</u> automobile Stuart had ever seen.*

    What does *miniature* mean in this sentence?
    - ○ a. able to be driven
    - ○ b. capable of becoming invisible
    - ○ c. capable of going fast
    - ○ d. much smaller than the usual size

14. *"Because this automobile is a thoroughly modern car. It's not only noiseless, it's <u>invisible</u>."*

    What is the car other than quiet?
    - ○ a. It's covered in neon.
    - ○ b. It can't be seen.
    - ○ c. It's unstoppable.
    - ○ d. It's easy to see.

15. *"Feel around for it."*
    So Stuart felt around until his hand came in <u>contact</u> with a button.

    What did Stuart's hand do?
    - ○ a. It touched a button.
    - ○ b. It stuck to a button.
    - ○ c. It slid off a button.
    - ○ d. It went away from a button.

16. *And so he and Stuart sat down and waited <u>patiently</u> until they no longer heard any crashing sounds in the room.*

How did Dr. Carey and Stuart wait for the car to stop?

- ○ a. like patients in a waiting room
- ○ b. in a calm way
- ○ c. very anxiously
- ○ d. by pacing the room

17. *You might think that writers get their ideas <u>automatically</u>. Actually, it takes time and work.*

What does *automatically* mean in the first sentence?

- ○ a. without much work
- ○ b. from other people
- ○ c. from books
- ○ d. with a lot of trouble

Score for Items 13–17 (x3) _______
15

4 WRITING AND LANGUAGE

18. Write one or two paragraphs about one of the topics below.

   a. What's the most unbelievable — but true — thing you've ever seen or read about? Explain why it seems unbelievable.

   b. Stuart may need another way to travel now that the car is wrecked. Write a description of another unbelievable method of transportation that he might use.

Rubric Score for Item 18 (x5) ______

20

19. Read the following book review. Find and correct nine
errors. Use what you know about proofreading to make
your corrections. The examples may help you. There are
four spelling errors, two adverb errors, two prepositional
phrase errors, and one error in using negatives.

Believe Me, You'll Love This Book!

Would you believe an island made of soap, a fish that is fast_^^{er} than
a cheetah, or a family with 100 children? You'll find this and more in
Carol Webber's new book, *Strange But True.*

I haven't~~'t~~ never read a book that contains so many fascinating
facts. My aunt gave the book to my brother and I. We didn't have
no idea how entertaining it would be. *Strange But True* contains
countles examples of amazing people and things from around the
world. Not a single fact is intrue.

Miss Webber says that putting the book together was a huge
project for she. It took five years to gather the information. "I
researched this book more carefullyer than any other," she says.

Strange But True will impress you with its unbelievable stories
from distunt lands. This is exactley the kind of book to take to the
beach. I read the whole book in one morning. My brother also read
it quick. We believe you'll enjoy it too!

Score for Item 19 _______
9

Choose the pair of sentences that use pronouns most clearly.

20. ○ a. They said they weren't afraid of the spooky house. Meghan and Shara walked past it.

    ○ b. They said they weren't afraid of the spooky house. They walked past it.

    ○ c. Meghan and Shara said they weren't afraid of the spooky house. Meghan and Shara walked past the spooky house.

    ○ d. Meghan and Shara said they weren't afraid of the spooky house. They walked past it.

21. ○ a. They were eager to test it out. They took their flashlight and walked toward it.

    ○ b. A shade fluttered in the window. It was broken.

    ○ c. A bat flew over the girls' heads. It gave a loud screech.

    ○ d. They dropped the flashlight. It circled overhead.

Score for Items 20–21 (x4) _______

8

5 NEWSPAPER REPORT

As a newspaper reporter, you have been asked to fill out the news story below to tell how you felt about what you read in Do You *Believe* This?? Your answers should show that you have thought about what you have read.

Theme Selections

"La Bamba"

Willie Bea and the Time the Martians Landed
McBroom Tells the Truth
Trapped in Tar

Do You *Believe* This??

Date _______________________________

By _______________________________

    Today we finished our study of Do You *Believe* This?? This theme is about the possible and impossible.

    My opinion of this theme is

____

____

____

    My favorite story in this theme was

____

____

because _______________________________

____

____

____

Some things I learned about reality and fantasy are

____

____

____

____

____

____

Some new words I learned are

____

____

____

____